Quick Draw Cats and Dogs

KINGFISHER

How to use this book

1. Trace the grid opposite. You can use any size of paper as long as the grid proportions are the same as the one in this book. The grid squares will help you position your drawing and ensure the different stages are correctly scaled.

2. Use a light pencil line to draw. That way you can rub out the lines much more easily.

3. Copy the shapes in step one, then add the new shapes in step two and so on. As you add each step, your picture will begin to take shape.

4. When you have copied each step, rub out the extra lines from the earlier step – to eventually reveal the final shape (as shown in the final step).

5. Now colour in your finished picture.

As you become more confident, you may find that you don't need the grid squares any more. You may wish to add your own finishing touches to the illustrations, such as background plants, to create a scene.

Labrador

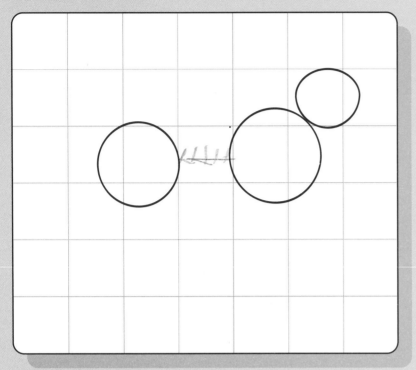

Step 1

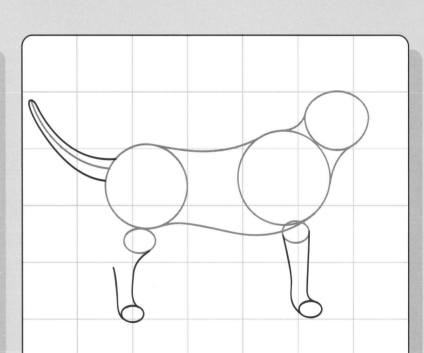

Step 2

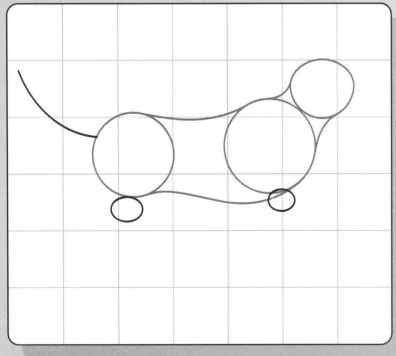

Step 3

Step 4

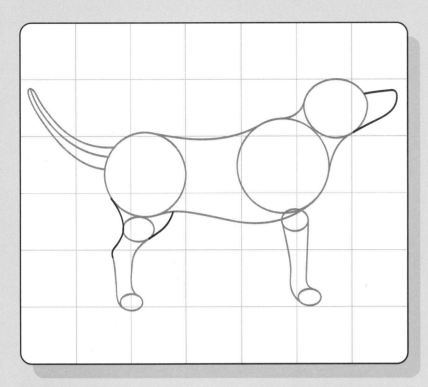

Step 5

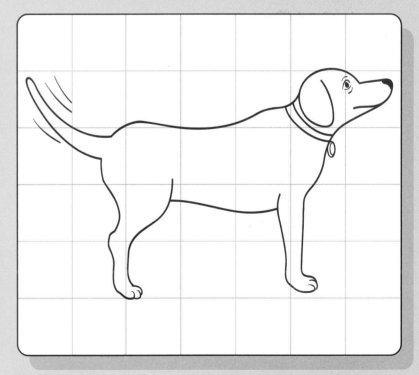

Step 6

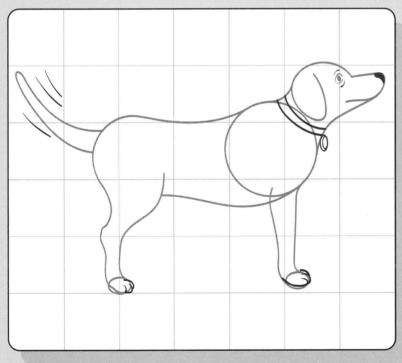

Step 7

Step 8

Prowling cat

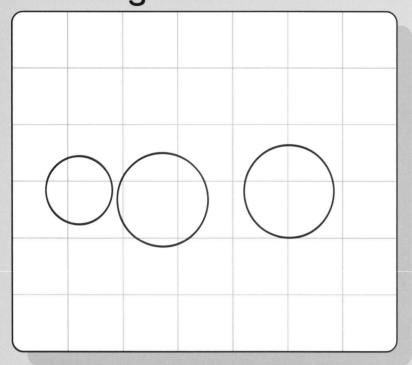

Step 1

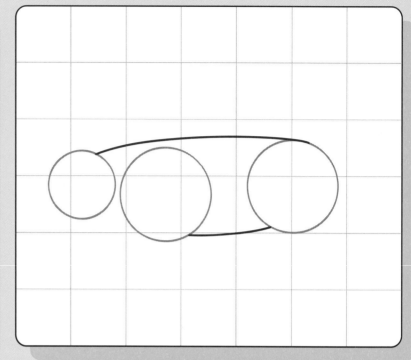

Step 2

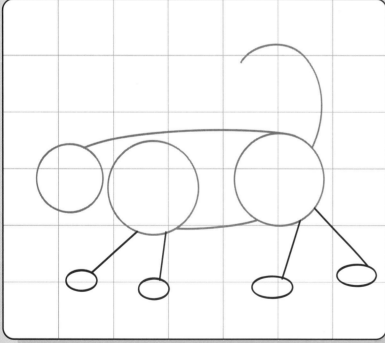

Step 3

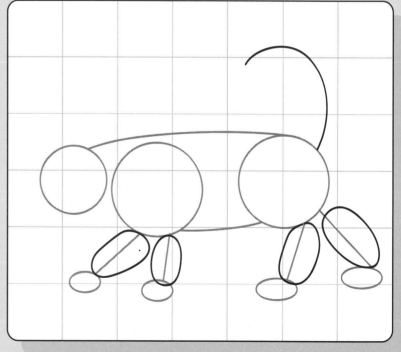

Step 4

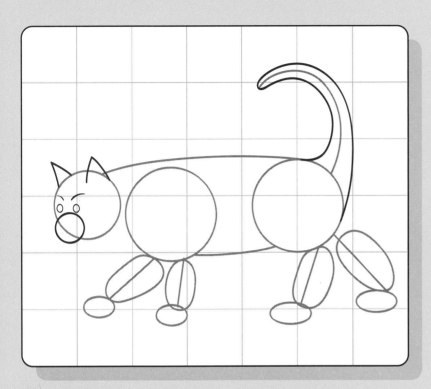

Step 5

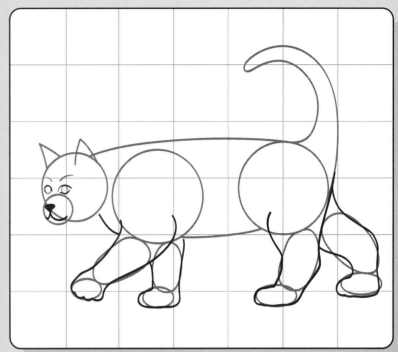

Step 6

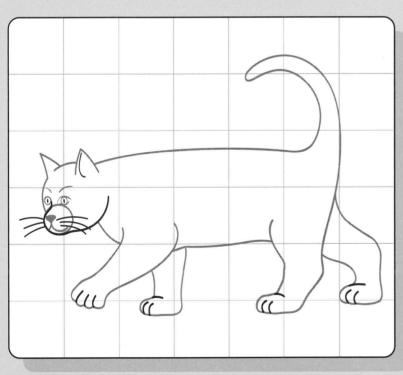

Step 7

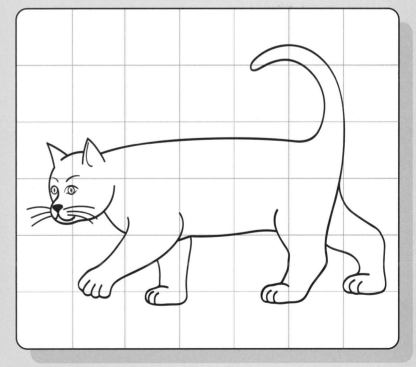

Step 8

Big dog

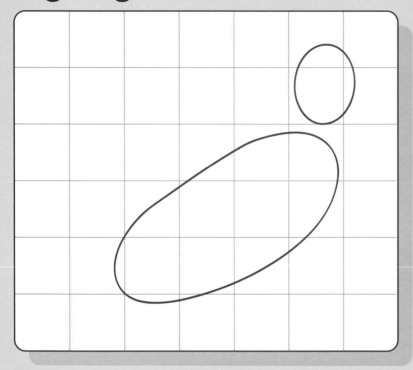

Step 1

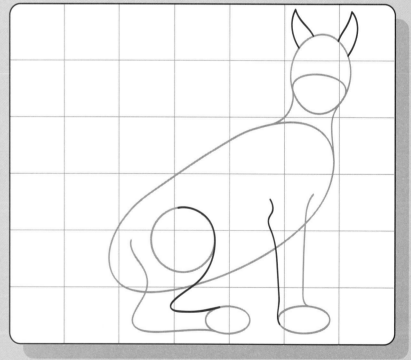

Step 2

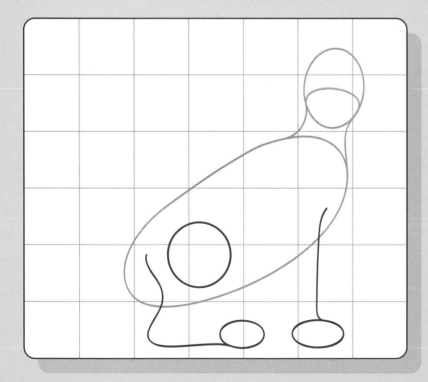

Step 3

Step 4

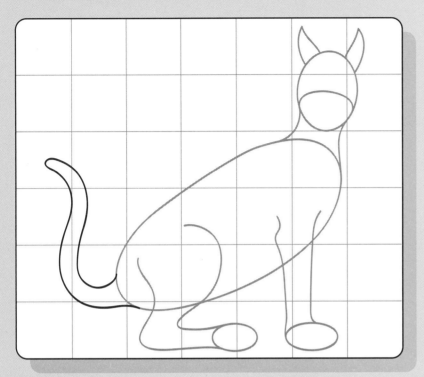

Step 5

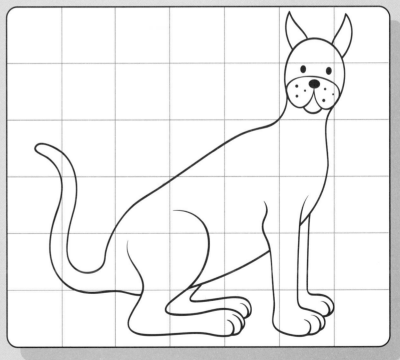

Step 6

Step 7

Step 8

Fat cat

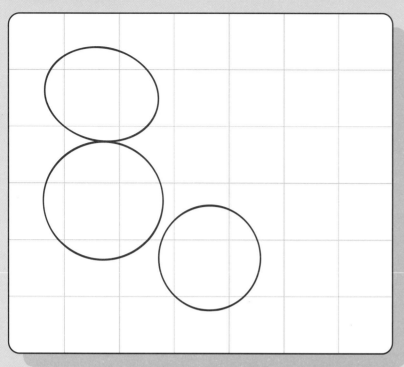

Step 1

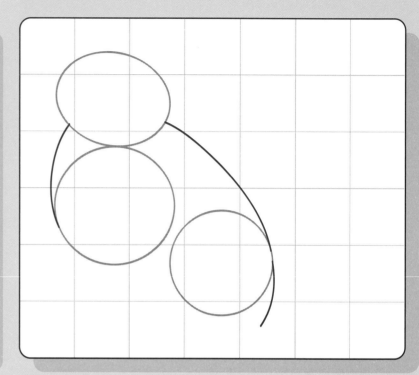

Step 2

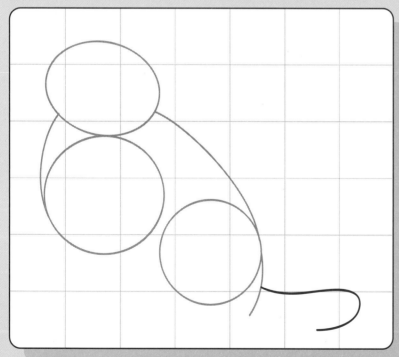

Step 3

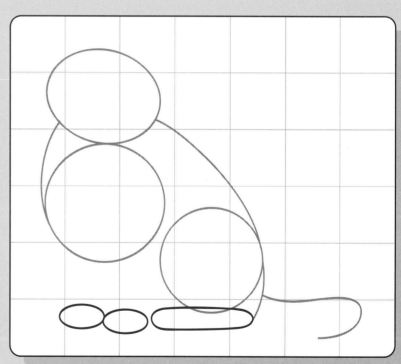

Step 4

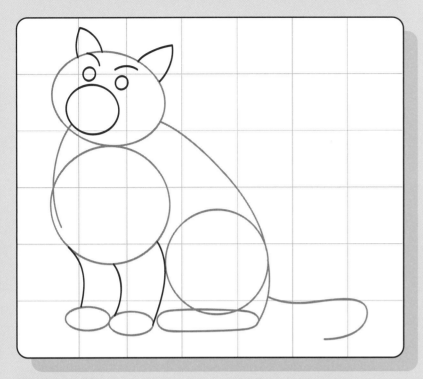

Step 5

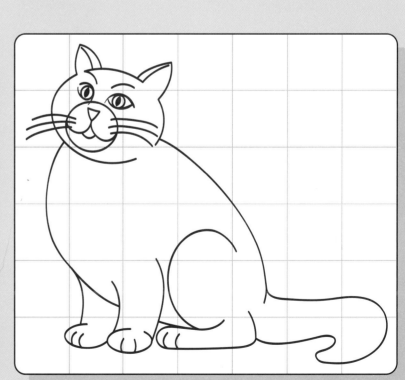

Step 6

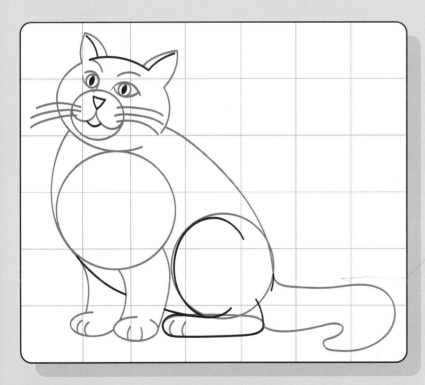

Step 7

Step 8

Puppy with a toy

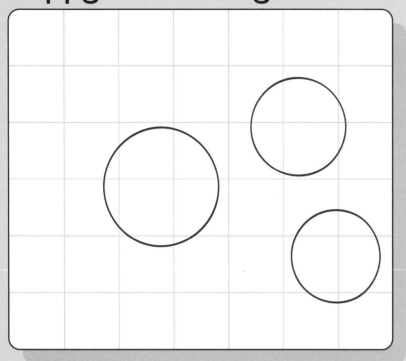

Step 1

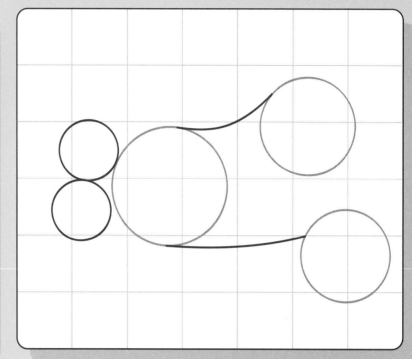

Step 2

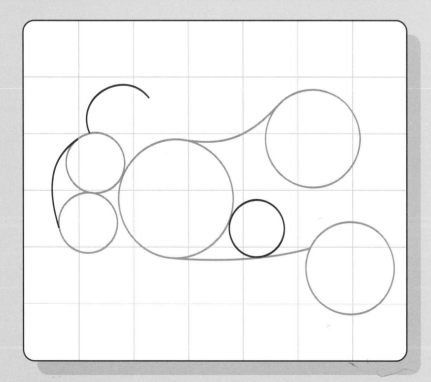

Step 3

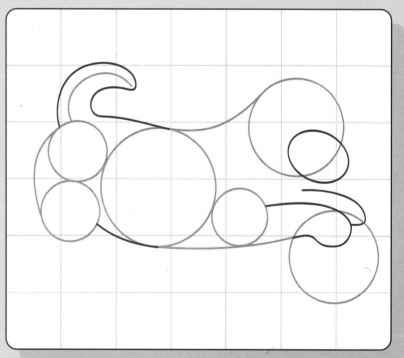

Step 4

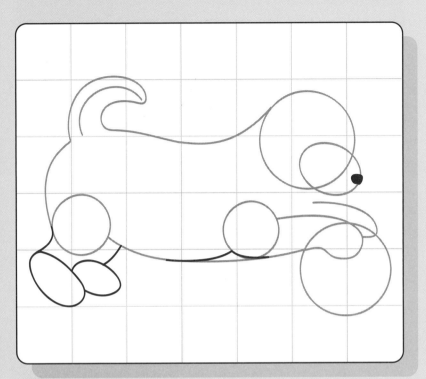

Step 5

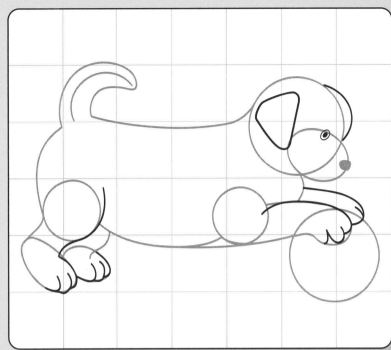

Step 6

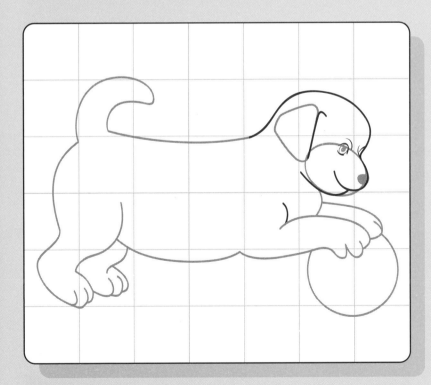

Step 7

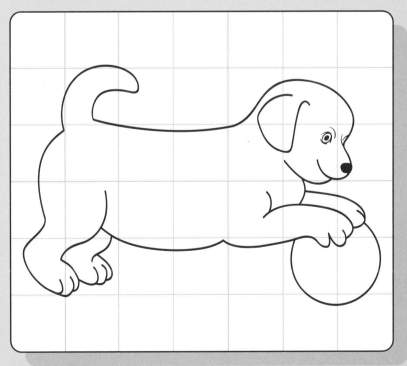

Step 8

Sleeping cat

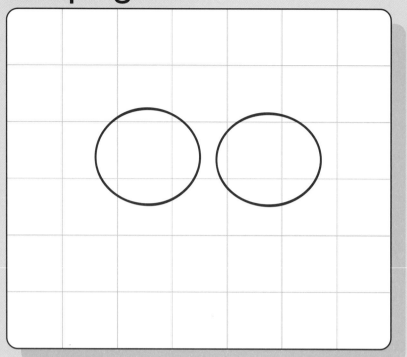

Step 1

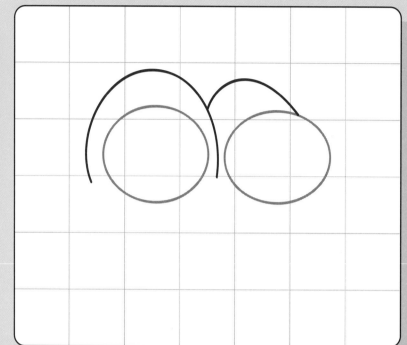

Step 2

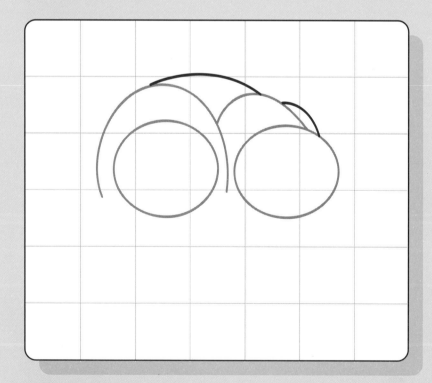

Step 3

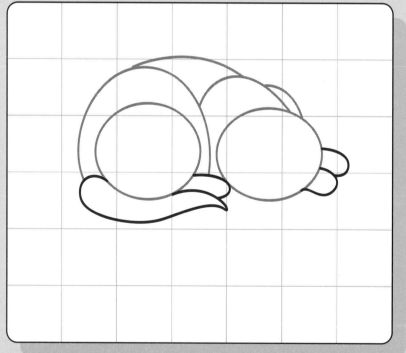

Step 4

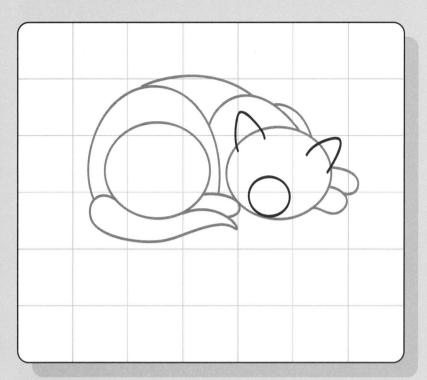

Step 5

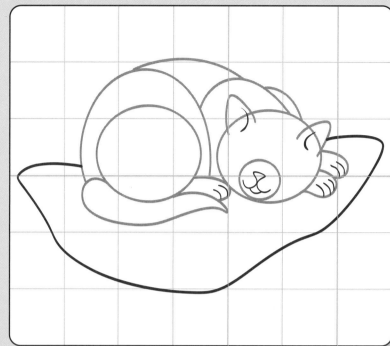

Step 6

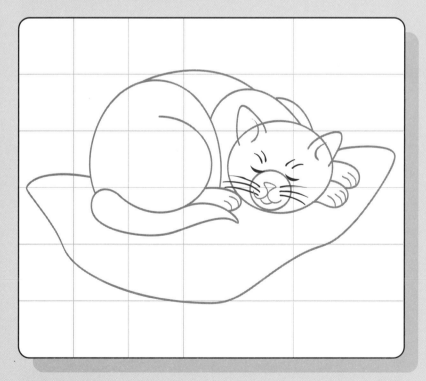

Step 7

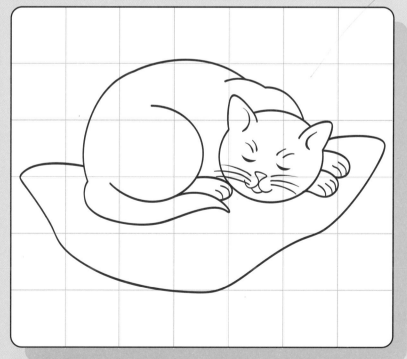

Step 8

Jack Russell

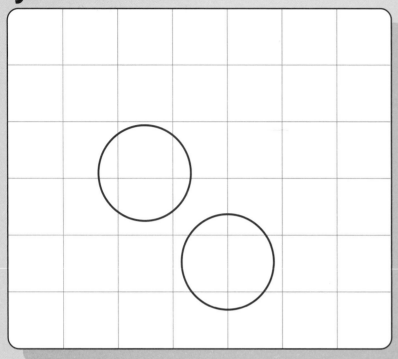

Step 1

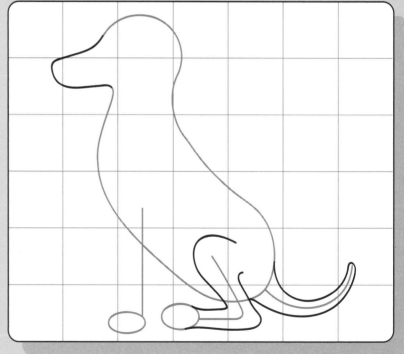

Step 2

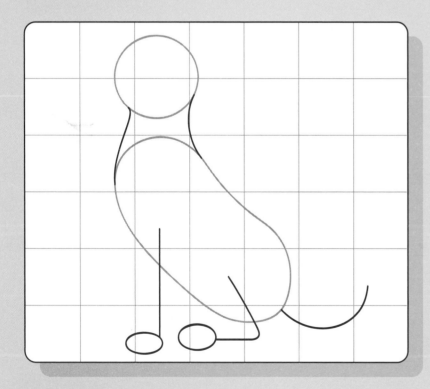

Step 3

Step 4

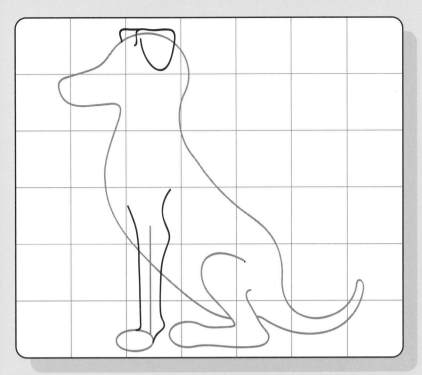

Step 5

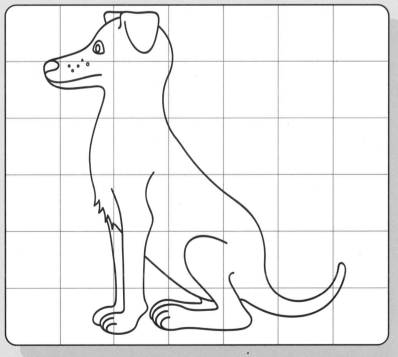

Step 6

Step 7

Step 8

Sitting cat

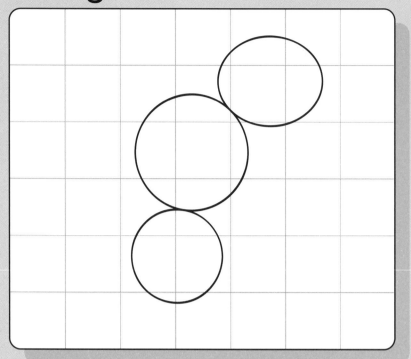

Step 1

Step 2

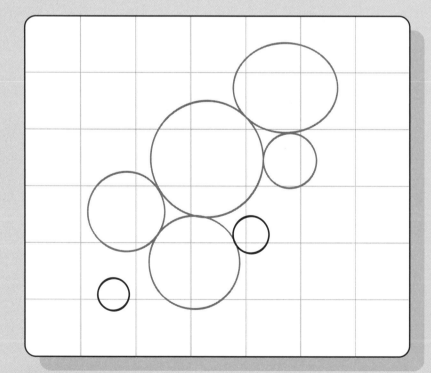

Step 3

Step 4

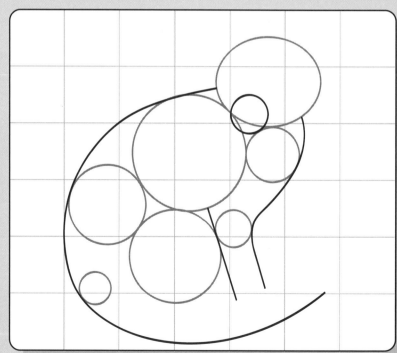

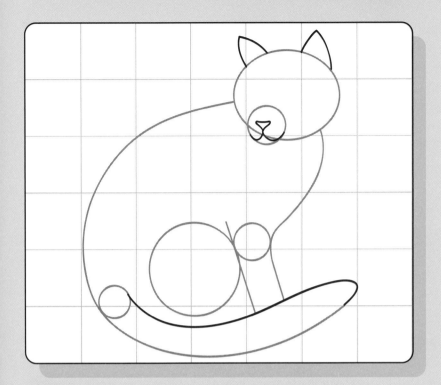

Step 5

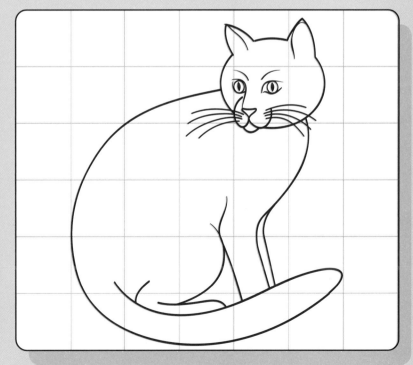

Step 6

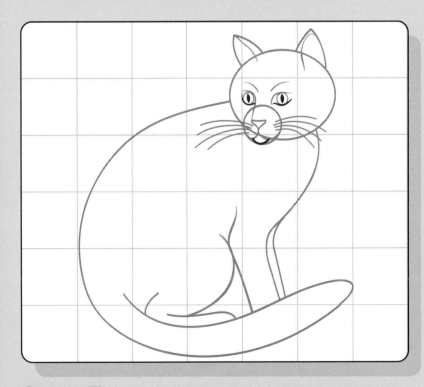

Step 7

Step 8

Dachshund

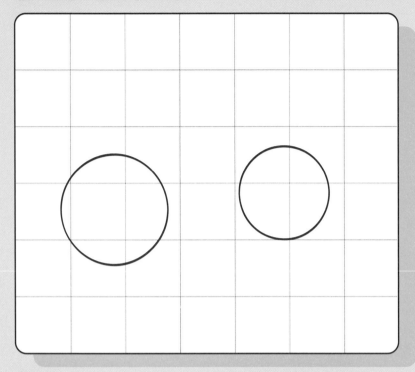

Step 1

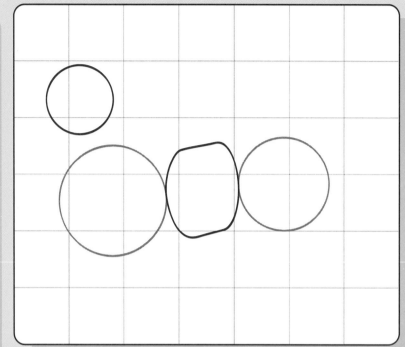

Step 2

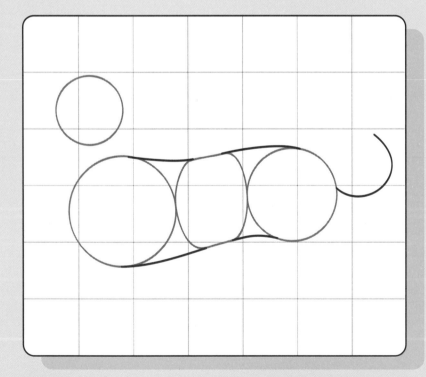

Step 3

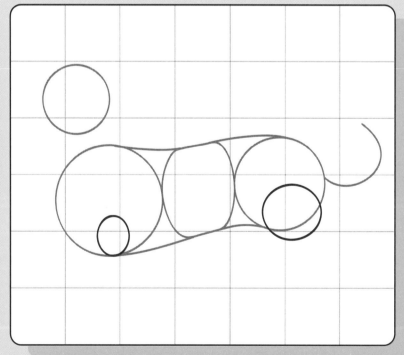

Step 4

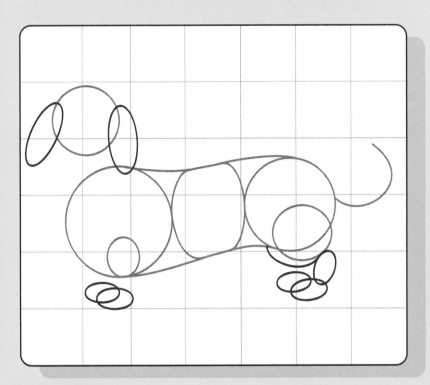

Step 5

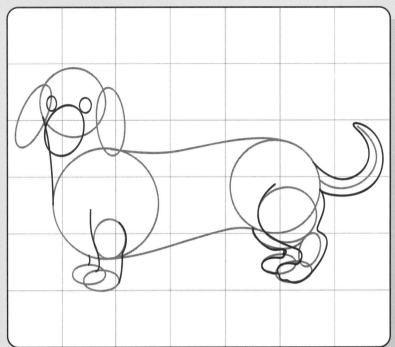

Step 6

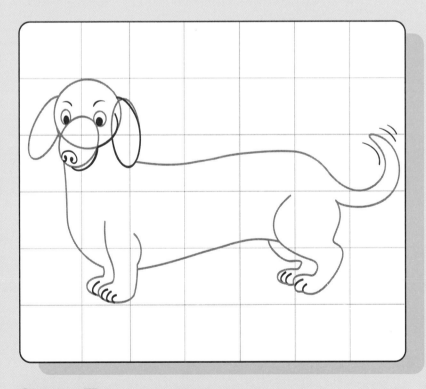

Step 7

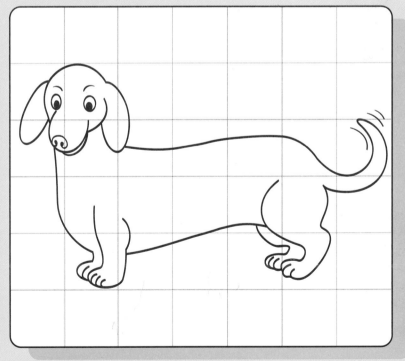

Step 8

Alley cat

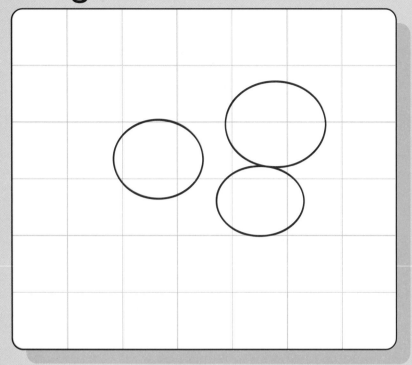

Step 1

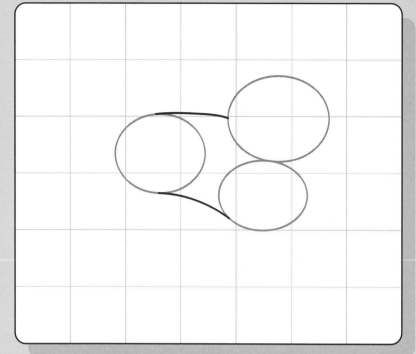

Step 2

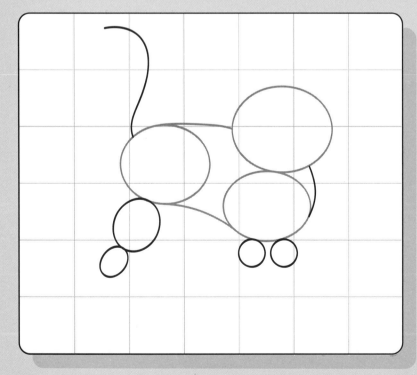

Step 3

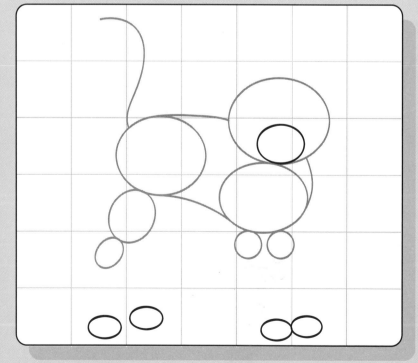

Step 4

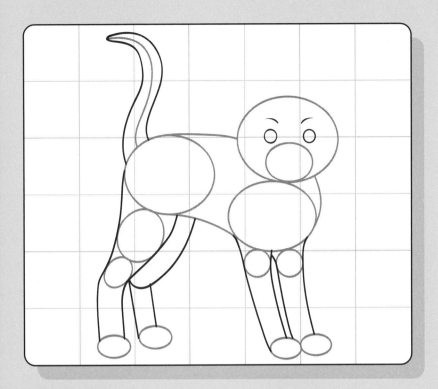

Step 5

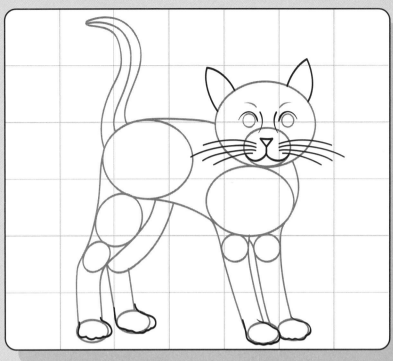

Step 6

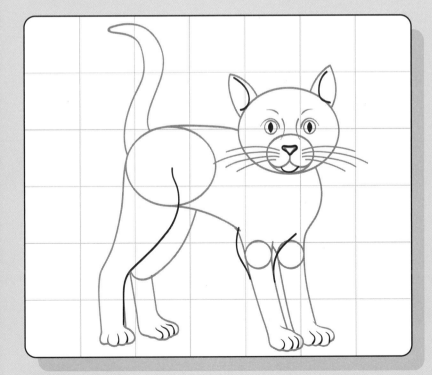

Step 7

Step 8

Dog begging for food

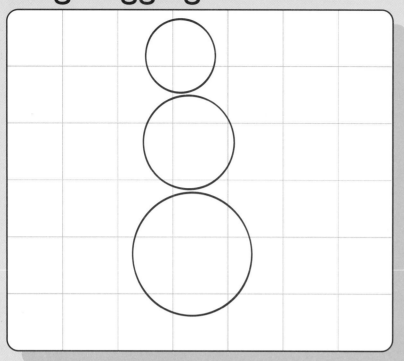

Step 1

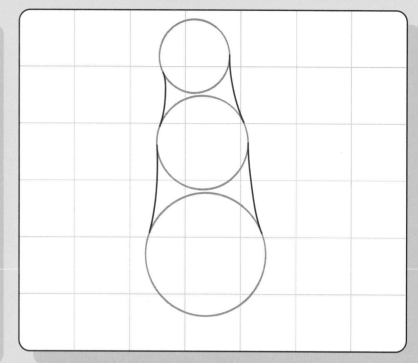

Step 2

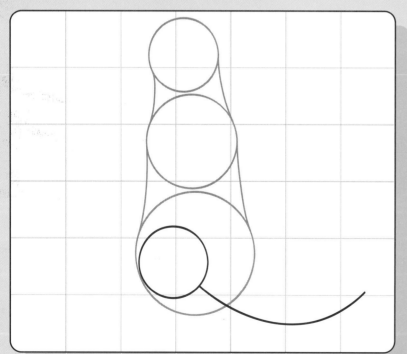

Step 3

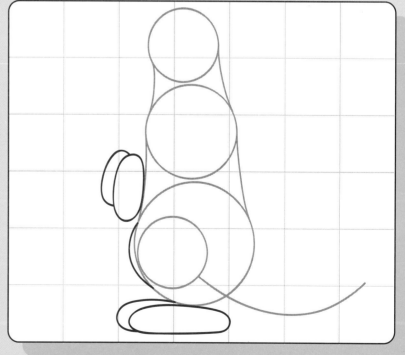

Step 4

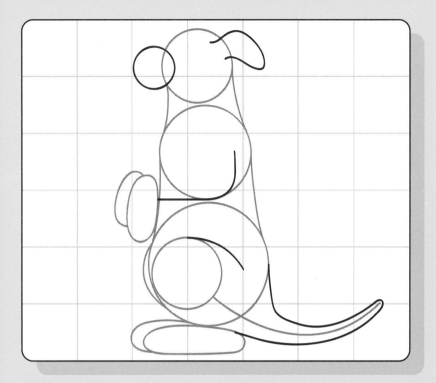

Step 5

Step 6

Step 7

Step 8

Kitten with a toy

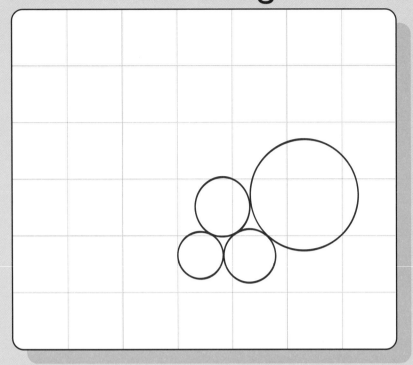

Step 1

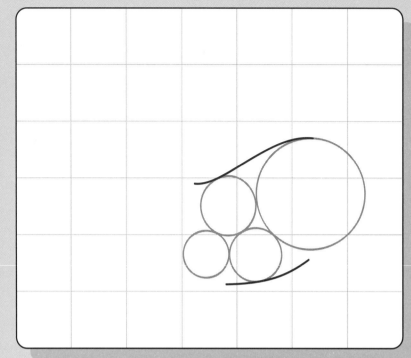

Step 2

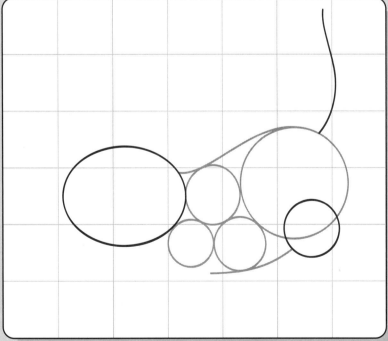

Step 3

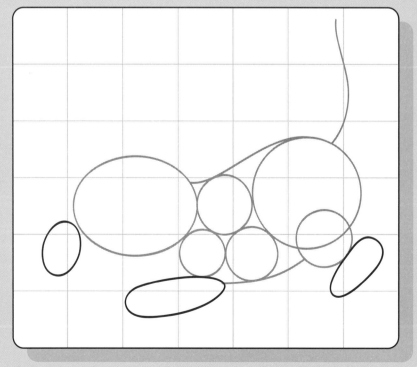

Step 4

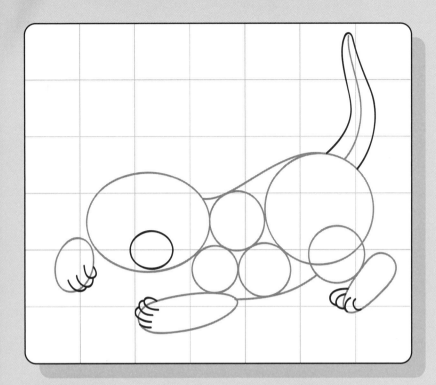

Step 5

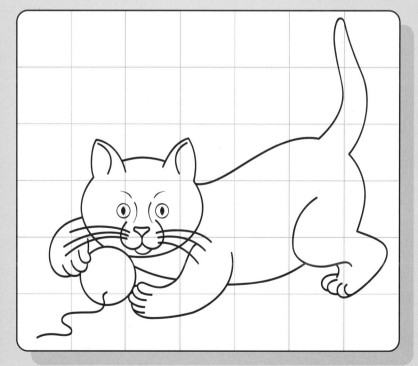

Step 6

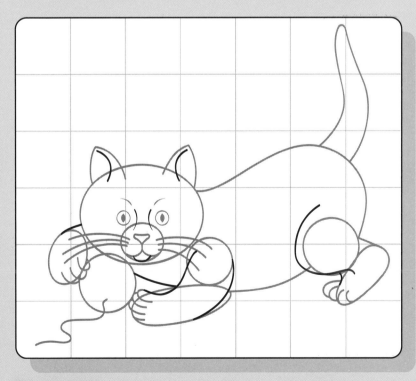

Step 7

Step 8

Greyhound

Step 1

Step 2

Step 3

Step 4

Step 5

Step 6

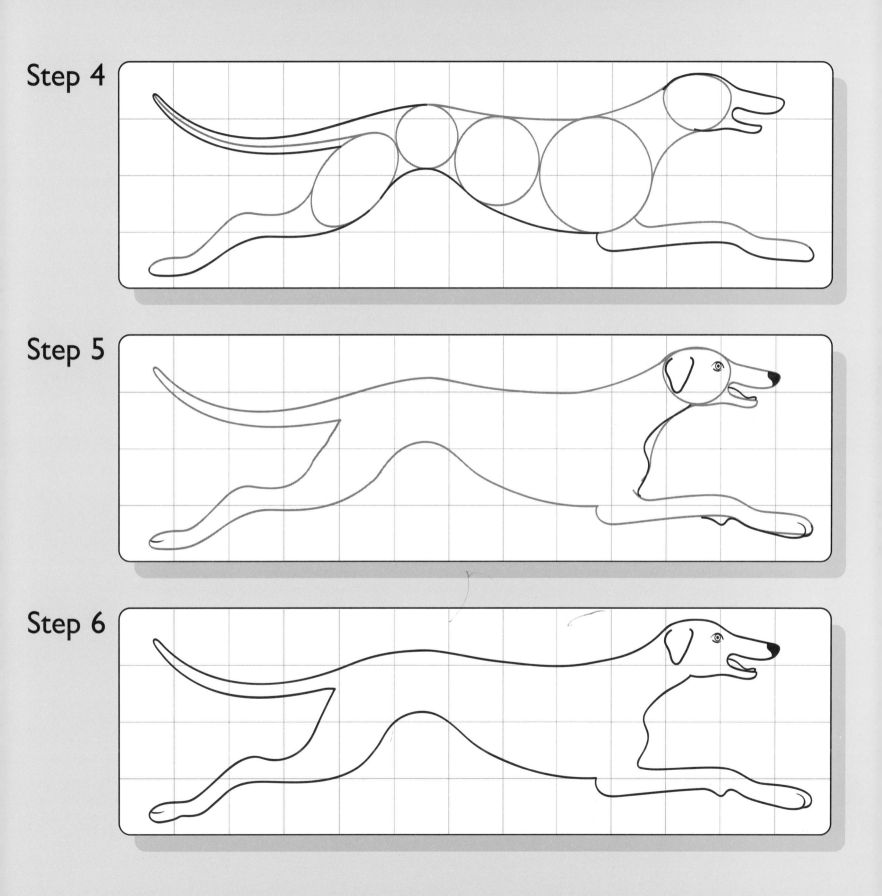

Cat and mouse

Step 1

Step 2

Step 3

Step 4

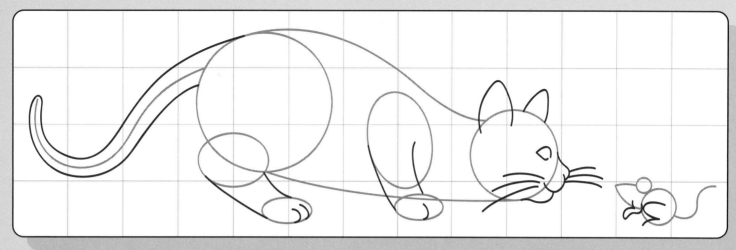

Step 5

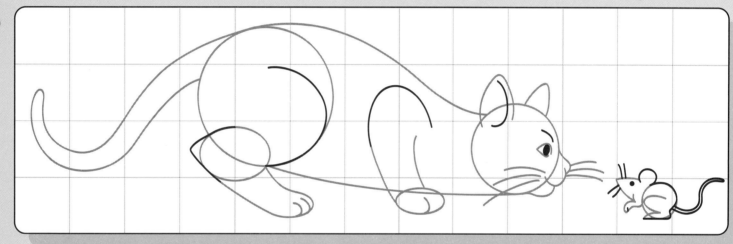

Step 6

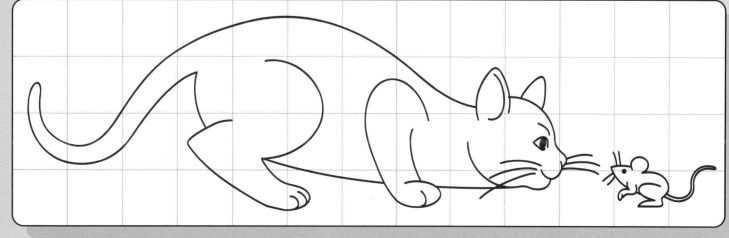

KINGFISHER

Kingfisher Publications Plc
New Penderel House
283–288 High Holborn
London WC1V 7HZ
www.kingfisherpub.com

First published by Kingfisher Plc 2007
10 9 8 7 6 5 4 3 2 1

TS/0707/PROSP/IGS/120WOF/C

ISBN 978 0 7534 1611 2

Produced for Kingfisher by The Peter Bull Art Studio

For Kingfisher:
Associate Creative Director: Mike Davis
Designers: Ray Bryant and Emy Manby
Senior production controller: Jessamy Oldfield
DTP Manager: Nicky Studdart

A CIP catalogue record for this book is available from
the British Library.

Printed in China